Daily Spiritual Striving

Torkom Saraydarian

Daily Spiritual Striving

© 1997 The Creative Trust

All Rights Reserved

No part of this publication may be reproduced, stored in a retrieval system, or transmitted in any form, by any means, electronic, mechanical, photocopying, recording or otherwise, without permission in writing from the copyright owner or his representatives.

ISBN: 0-929874-57-9

Library of Congress Catalog Card Number: 96-61706

Printed in the United States of America

Printed By: KNI Incorporated, Anaheim, CA

Published By: T.S.G. Publishing Foundation, Inc.
P. O. Box 7068
Cave Creek, AZ 85327-7068 USA

NOTE: The exercises and meditations given in this book should be used only after receiving professional advice.

All excerpts reprinted by permission of The Creative Trust. All rights reserved.

Contents

I   A Daily Discipline of Worship 5

II   Prayer 13

III   Purification 19

IV   The Great Invocation 29

V   The Gayatri 39

VI   The Lord's Prayer 55

    Index 71

This booklet contains reprints from several of Torkom Saraydarian's books on the subject of daily spiritual practices. The topics included are prayer, invocations, purifications as well as a discussion of *The Lord's Prayer*, *The Great Invocation,* and *The Gayatri*.

These prayers and mantrams have offered deep solace and comfort to millions of people throughout centuries.

- Publisher -

I

A Daily Discipline of Worship

There is a rhythm in the flow of the energies in Nature. Those who are sensitive and can enter into the rhythm demonstrate a greater power of survival and creativity. One of the methods to enter into the rhythm of Nature is the daily discipline of five-pointed worship.

People forget about worship in their daily problems, interests, activities, loves and hates, labors and pleasures; and eventually they turn into machines. When people forget to contact daily the Divine Presence in the whole of Nature, they slowly turn into machines, and the changes and events of life control them. Their blind urges and drives, their vanity and ego control them. They turn into a board of push buttons and they lose control over their own lives.

When a person turns into a board of push buttons or a machine, he loses the direction of his life. This is the situation with the majority of the people in the world. People who lose their life's direction are called "orphans" or people who have no guidance or protection.

Daily contact with the Presence is not the reading of religious books, the singing of hymns, or even listening to sermons. It is a real, heartfelt contact with the Presence that expands your consciousness, makes you pure, sincere, and fearless, and creates in you a spirit of striving toward perfection.

Hypocrisy and the evil associated with it come into being when people speak about religion and pretend that they are religious while having no real contact with the Presence. To keep the needle of our life's compass pointed in the right direction, we need to set the compass right five times daily. If the needle is not set right, no matter what you think, speak, or do, it creates reverse results in your life.

In order to set the needle of your compass in the right direction, you need to have contact with the Highest through your worship. Daily worship is divided into five parts. If people follow this five-pointed worship daily:

1. They minimize the pain and suffering in their lives.
2. They create a better world.
3. They understand to a greater extent the laws of life and Nature.
4. They become more creative.
5. They re-spiritualize themselves.

Worship is a technique to contact the Highest that your heart can reach. In practicing the five-pointed daily discipline of worship, you bring great changes in your life, even within a month.

The first moment of worship takes place early in the morning, immediately before sunrise, when you can hear the marvelous symphony of hundreds of birds. How can this be practiced?

Early in the morning, after you clean yourself, sit in a comfortable place at home or in Nature. Relax, breathe deeply, and after concentrating your mind in the center of your heart, say with real aspiration:

> *O Giver of Light,*
> *the Cosmic Beauty,*
> *permeate my whole nature*
> *with Thy Rays.*
> *Kindle the flame*
> *on the altar of*
> *my temple*
> *so that I may live*
> *as a beam of light,*
> *in beauty,*
> *until the sunset*
> *of the day . . .*
> *of my life.*

Then meditate on the above words for ten or fifteen minutes and start your daily life. This can be done between 5:00 and 6:00 a.m., or earlier. Remember that beauty is the most powerful force in the Universe.

This contact may change your life and disperse ugly thoughts from your mind, ugly words from your mouth, ugly feelings from your heart, and ugly actions from your body. It may restore beauty in all your expressions and make you extremely magnetic. But you must be sincere and real in your appeal for beauty.

The second point of worship starts at 9:00 a.m. It is possible that you may be busy with many things. Never mind. Take a few minutes for a break. Concentrate your mind, raise your heart toward the Great Presence, and say:

> *O Sphere of Light,*
> *advancing and elevating Goodness,*
> *may my soul*
> *rise with You,*
> *expressing goodness*
> *in all its contacts.*

Then meditate for two or three minutes about how your life can turn into a radiant goodness in all your contacts.

This is a very simple discipline to build a contact with the Presence and act inspired by the Presence. Most of us depend upon what we know, what we have, what we can do; we depend on our position, power, money, and titles. All these things upon which we depend are like the false walls that people use to trap elephants: the hunters build false walls in the forest, or they erect uprooted tree trunks, and the elephants come and lean on them to go to sleep, then suddenly fall. Once they fall, the hunters come and catch them. Thus, our vanities, ego, position, possessions, wealth, and power are like these walls that we build to trap *ourselves.* The only thing that we must depend upon, if we want security and protection, is the Great Presence, the Great Spirit—God.

The third point of worship is at noon. It can take two or three minutes, or more if you have time. You withdraw into your being and focus your consciousness on the flame of life within your heart center and say:

> *The flame of the Great Presence*
> *in me,*
> *let me stand*
> *as a radiant fire*
> *of righteousness*
> *today*
> *and during the days*
> *of my life.*
> *Let me think, act, and speak*
> *in the spirit*
> *of righteousness.*

Then keep silent for a few minutes to meditate upon what you said, and in your creative imagination see the spirit of righteousness operating all over the world.

Invoking righteousness may change the whole course of your life. As the Sun rises in the sky at 12:00 noon, your spirit of righteousness can rise within you and spread righteousness through all your thinking, judgments, and actions. Righteousness creates stability in your consciousness and in your direction of life. Righteous people survive in very tempting and crucial conditions.

The fourth point of worship is at sunset. Sit down—if possible in Nature or under a tree—withdraw into your being, and say:

> *My Lord,*
> *thank You for the joy*
> *of living today*
> *in the spirit of beauty,*
> *goodness,*
> *and righteousness.*
> *May Your joy*
> *radiate in other parts of the world*
> *as the Sun*
> *disperses the night*
> *and brings the joy of the day.*
> *My Lord,*
> *You are the joy of my heart.*

Then for five to ten minutes meditate about how grateful you are for being beautiful all day, for being full of goodness all day, for being righteous all day. Feel that your heart is now full of joy because you tried to live by divine standards. Fill your whole being with joy. Let joy radiate from your whole being. Joyfully express your gratitude for living today in His Presence.

For those who live a life of crime, hatred, deception, exploitation, killing, malice, slander, treason, stealing, and lying, the day is full of sorrow, pain and suffering. But your day will be a day of joy because you lived in your highest vision.

The fifth point of worship is before sleep. Imagine in what conditions people in general sleep: in fear, in anxiety, in pain. Some are drunk; some are angry and hateful. Some go to sleep in tears, depression, or resentment. Some go to sleep after criminal acts. But you are going to sleep in peace because all day you were beautiful; you were full of goodness; you were righteous; you were joyful.

To go to sleep means to enter the gates of the Higher Worlds. The world of matter, the world of conflict and selfish interests, must be left behind, and you must have peace in your heart in order to enter the gates leading your soul to Higher Worlds. If you enter the Higher Worlds, the principles and laws of the Higher Worlds will make an overhaul of your psychic machine and adjust your whole mechanism according to higher directions. When people cannot enter the Higher Worlds, they do not receive any psychic repair and their machine degenerates itself and adapts itself to the transient interests of the world.

Worship means to have power to live according to your spiritual ideals, and you can cultivate the power of your worship through such a discipline.

At the time of sleep, sit on your bed, relax yourself with a spirit of gratitude, and say:

> *My Lord, let Your freedom*
> *permeate my whole being.*
> *Let me be free*
> *from all worries and anxieties,*
> *from all painful memories of the day,*
> *from all attachments and identifications,*
> *so that my soul freely soars*
> *in Your temple of beauty.*
> *Let me realize freedom*

> *from my physical,*
> *emotional, and mental crystallizations*
> *and be with You as a free soul.*

Visualize the hands of the Lord upon your head, and go to sleep in peace.

When you sleep in such peace, you will see how your mind will be free from all limitations of dogma, doctrines, formulas, crystallized prejudices and superstitions, and it will soar like an eagle in the presence of the One Who is everywhere and in everything. Free people are those people who are free from their own limitations, hang-ups, and identifications.

You cannot make people free. They must make themselves free by their own efforts. Freedom can be accomplished by outgrowing your limitations and slavery. A slave of the body, vices, and habits; a slave of ego, vanity, and power will never experience freedom, and if you give him freedom, he will destroy himself.

True freedom can only be gained through the process of transfiguration of life. Freedom after sleep must be experienced in order to have an idea of what true freedom is. You can achieve such a state of freedom after detaching yourself from the shores of self-interest and opening your sails to the winds of the Great Presence.

One may ask why it is better to go to sleep with peace and joy than in an intoxicated manner, full of dope, or hatred, revenge, jealousy, or thoughts of crime. Sleep is given to us to regenerate our spiritual mechanism so that we come back to our daily consciousness with feelings of beauty, goodness, justice, joy, and freedom.

Most of our dreams come from our sexual fantasies, our filled stomachs, our anxieties, fears, desires, worries, expectations, and hatreds. Real dreams are guidance and revelations. We can have such dreams if we go to sleep in the right way, detaching our soul from the glamors of earthly life. The moment of sleep must be a moment of initiation into Higher Worlds.

You will see that this procedure is a five-pointed star of worship through Beauty, Goodness, Righteousness, Joy, and Freedom, which will change your whole life. If you keep this five-pointed contact for one year, you will see a great improvement in your health, prosperity, social relations, spiritual development, and spiritual contact with Higher Worlds.

Prosperity is the result of an elevating consciousness. If you gain money by exploiting and cheating people, that money does not belong to you, and it will create more pain than joy in you. Through this five-pointed worship you attract those energies and forces that help you to be in abundance. Remember the words of Christ: "Be courageous because I overcame the world." Courage is the ability to break your mechanical way of living. You need courage to start this discipline.

Thus you follow the course of the Sun: the sunrise—beauty; the elevation of the Sun—goodness; the zenith of the Sun—righteousness; the decline of the Sun—joy; the sunset—the mystery of freedom. If you continue to live through this five-pointed worship, you will turn into a *Son of Light*.

A Daily Discipline of Worship

II

Prayer

Prayer is a dialogue between you, the human soul and your Inner Guide, between the disciple and Master, between the disciple and Christ, between the disciple and Planetary, Solar, or Cosmic Beings, or between the disciple and the Almighty Presence in the Universe.

Some of us do not care for prayers, but in esoteric literature we find that not only individuals pray, but also Masters pray, and the Ones Who are greater than Masters pray. For example, Christ prayed.

Our prayer changes according to our level of consciousness. As the level of our consciousness rises, our needs change and the intensity of our demand grows.

Man prays in different ways. For example, if you desire something, in a sense you are praying. People pray also through aspiration, dedication, and creativity. You can pray in an intuitive way or use your willpower to demand, which is prayer on atmic levels.

It is very interesting to know that whatever you desire, you will get. That is the law of Nature, the root of freedom and bondage. Your prayer will be answered, perhaps not immediately, but eventually—in one life or after two hundred lives.

Needs can be seen more clearly if you are conscious on higher planes. If you are in the physical plane consciousness, you always pray for physical objects and you mostly say, "Give me, give me, give me!"

If your consciousness is elevated to higher levels you ask for peace on earth, goodwill for every man, beauty, enlightenment, and so on. It is your level that decides the objects you are asking for.

Prayers are based on the law of invocation and evocation. The one who prays puts many forces and energies into action in the Universe. The machine of the Universe operates and eventually fills the order you placed. It happens sometimes that the object that comes to you is already obsolete, but it is yours; you ordered it.

According to the Ageless Wisdom, all that comes to you is all that you asked for. Sometimes we receive things we never wanted, but in a moment of excitement or madness we put in an order, and the law of the Universe answers our request. We then receive it whether we like it or not.

It happens sometimes that you order things for which you are not ready. One of my friends wanted to be the chairman of an organization. After a few years he became chairman, but he started to curse his position and tried to find ways and means to get out of it.

Another friend was crazy to be a millionaire. One day he won a sweepstakes, but a few days later, they took him to an asylum because he lost control of his mind. You must pray for things that you can handle when they materialize.

There are also prayers that work diametrically opposite to your evolution when they are answered. You ask for boyfriends or girlfriends, and they start coming into your life in such abundance that you lose your time, your head, and your sanity. They come abundantly because you made such a wild demand for them.

Sometimes at the time we desire and pray we feel a rejection from within us. This is a very subtle indication that within us there is a Presence that is warning us not to pray for certain things or not to desire certain things. That Inner Presence sees that when our prayer is answered, it will be a punishment, not a gift. We can call this inner rejection, the Conscience, or the Voice of our Heart, or the suggestion of our Inner Guide. This means that we must be careful when we place an order to the Great Presence.

I know a boy who was very eager to use hashish, and life brought him a little bag of hashish. He called his friends to his home. They built a nice fire and began to dope themselves. Eventually they were found burned to death after the whole house caught fire.

People often pray for things for their own destruction. Man has the freedom to ask or to pray for whatever he wants. Such a choice may lead him toward destruction or toward achievement. Your future is what you ask for or pray for. It is just like a department store when you go and ask for something. They say that in two days it will be ready, but then it reaches you in two months because the store had to order it for you. They ordered it from Europe. Then the post office ripped the address and other obstructions appeared. All these things delayed your order, although eventually you did receive it.

Again, the most important thing is to be careful of what you order through your prayers. In our ordinary life we sometimes order things we can't even use, or do not have space for, or it is too late to have them, or they become the biggest headache of our life. It is very interesting that we buy our troubles with our desires or prayers. Desire creates a great vacuum in our aura and puts a demand on the universal laws to fill that vacuum. That is why Christ said, "Ask and it will be given to you."

Often we interfere and delay or hasten the answer to our

prayers. For example, a doubt will delay the answer for years or lives. An inaccuracy in our demand will bring the parts that we cannot use for our motor. That is why we must know exactly what we want. If we order the wrong part, we will receive exactly what we ordered. When it comes it will not fit the car.

Then we have aspiration. Aspiration brings development, unfoldment in your nature; more health, more beauty, more light, and more goodness. This is a way to clean yourself of objects of desire.

In desire you always want *to have*. In aspiration you mostly strive *to be*. In aspiration you admire something and it raises your level once you try to strive toward it.

Next we have devotion. Devotion is not only asking but also giving. You slowly lose your identity in the image to which you devote yourself, but you receive the fusion of the image with yourself. You slowly renounce all your belongings and selfishness, and you live only in the object of devotion.

In devotion you slowly come in contact with your Inner Guide. Here again we say that your devotion is relative to your level of consciousness. If your consciousness is higher, the object of your devotion is higher, and the effect is the response from higher sources.

The next form of prayer is creativity. Creativity is the state of consciousness in which you enter into the treasury of your innermost being and bring the beauty into manifestation. You come in contact with the glories of the Great Presence and bring those glories out into manifestation in your creative work. The creative moment is the moment of contact with that frequency in you which reveals the mystery of colors, sound, movements, and symbols. In creativity, you answer your own need; you meet your own need.

Creativity starts first with imagination. You want something and you produce or imagine it. The simplest example is when a cat plays with a piece of cloth as if it were a mouse, as if the mouse were in its paws.

The next stage is visualization, in which you have direct manipulation of the laws of thought and mental force. Through these laws you bring into manifestation things which will be a great blessing for humanity.

Thus creativity is a contact with prototypes and the ability to bring them into manifestation. In the course of such a process, you eventually confront the task of creating yourself anew, and you let that Self manifest in its highest glory. This is how you may be born again spiritually.

There are even higher levels of prayer or dialogue. Intuitive prayer is direct contact with the One Presence. Here you receive all that you want to further the evolution of humanity, and your life turns into a great service.

In the next degree we have Atmic prayer. This is actually a process of fusing your will with the Will of the Great Presence when you say, "Father, not my will but Thine be done." This is the moment when you renounce all that you asked for, all that you had, all that you were, and become one with the Will of the "Father."

The Psyche and Psychism, pp. 841-844.

III

Purification

Purification is a painful process, due to the fact that the substances of your body, emotions, and mind are fused with elements of impurity, whether they are physical, emotional, or mental. Due to this fusion, the process of separation, or the removal of that impure element, causes pain because the element does not want to come out or the vehicle is in some way stuck to it.

For example, pulling out a thorn in your finger or toe is painful. Cutting a tumor out is painful. The cleaning of microbes from your body is painful. Pulling out a decayed tooth is painful.

The same thing is true of the emotional nature. You have glamors, desires, fears, depressive moods, negative emotions. All these elements are impressed upon the emotional body, imported or self-developed. Removing these things from the emotional body initially creates emotional pain, and then, of course, a great release.

It is true also of the mental body. For example, pride, various vanities, selfishness, separativeness, illusions, prejudices, or superstition are elements which are rooted in our mental body as parasites. It is always painful to remove them, to destroy them, or to eliminate them in any way.

Essentially, within our threefold nature these impure elements are pain-producing factors or disorders and sickness-producing factors. That is why preventive action must not only be taken for the physical body but for the emotional and mental natures, too.

These impure elements create various problems in the process of elimination. For example, if they are not wiped away totally in the emotional nature, they will grow again and become malignant. Or the broken-up masses of impure elements will float within the emotional body and create various frictions around the centers and often hinder the energy circulation within the network of force channels.

A similar thing happens in the mental body. If the disintegrated thoughtforms are not eliminated totally, they may become revived, stimulated, and, because of the Law of Association, attract many similar pieces from space and form a more dangerous thoughtform.

There is also the problem of reactions of the bodies. Sometimes they enjoy impure elements, and if you remove them, they protest. The bodies do not want to give up impurities. Heavier demands to eliminate these elements create heavier reactions. The bodies even feel so strongly that they prevent the Soul from pulling impurities out of them. One of the examples of this is when a man is a drug addict. A habit is another form of protest. People even enjoy hating or killing others. This is a stage in which the cancer or hatred and crime is fully possessing the body or the organ.

Elimination of impurities needs time, skill-in-action, profound knowledge, and spiritual light. It is the same as an electrical system: when you turn on the switch, the electrical current flows down the wires. If you have a deteriorated portion of the wire, you have a short circuit.

It is known by many that before an organ or an emotional or mental nature is cured, it feels painful. A flash of pain appears; then the body is cured.

There is the life energy in our system. The blood is the physical expression of it. That is why blood is called "life." There is blood in the emotional and mental bodies that circulates in them, gives vitality, repairs the damages done by various means, attacks germs of emotional and mental kinds, and protects the mechanism. And if there are blockages on the path of its circulation, they create friction; they fight, leaving behind deteriorated elements that must be carried away, just as the white blood cells do a similar job in the body.

If the psychic energy does not circulate properly within the subtle bodies of the personality, it affects the blood circulation, and the blood loses its vitality and its ability to circulate properly.

Lack of trace minerals, different attacks of microbes, and so on make the blood weak and even pollute it.

Similar things happen with the psychic energy. Unhealthy emotional and mental conditions eventually weaken psychic energy, and because of this the mental, emotional, and physical natures deteriorate.

Pain is also created when the purified but weakened tissues on the three levels of the personality are exposed to vital energy beyond their capacity. When this vital energy is released, the sensitive tissue aches. This pain is translated in different bodies by different names.

When through some psychological exercises or through exercising our virtues, spiritual ideals, ideas, and visions we remove some hindrances from our nature, we feel sudden pain. If the counterpart of that hindrance is healed in the physical body or in the astral body, we feel a different pain and a still different pain in the mental realms. But after such a curing or healing pain, joy and health return.

Let us remember that wherever the circulation of vital energies is not in order, there are decay and attacks of various kinds. Some people speak about lack of honesty or morality. They are the same phenomena. In this condition, the psychic energy is not in circulation, and the emotional and mental natures are growing weeds, preventing the life-giving energies from bringing the message of light and love and power from our Inner Core, from our Inner Divinity.

The entire phenomena of pain, healing, and circulation of energy apply also to groups and nations. Groups and nations can have the same problems as an individual, but in greater magnitude. Groups and nations degenerate when the circulation of psychic energy is not free, or if they are not able to clean hindrances on their path in the group or national personality vehicles.

In reading the history of humanity, we see that past superpowers vanished because physical, emotional, and mental degeneration settled into their citizens and blocked their psychic energy. This situation passed from the individual to the group or national body. Love, light, and power, and also the sense of destiny and urge toward the future became blocked. Read the histories of the Aztec, Mayan, Roman, Chaldean, Babylonian, Byzantine, and Mongolian empires. They each vanished from earth for the same reason an individual degenerates and deteriorates physically, morally, and spiritually.

Individuals, groups, or nations that are living in the tension of fear, hatred, greed, and revenge eventually deteriorate physically, emotionally, and mentally because hatred blocks life energy. Greed and fear do the same thing; jealousy and revenge burn the protective nets of the aura. The defeat and degeneration of nations start the moment life energies begin to be blocked. It is the same with every kind of organism. Any blockage within an individual eventually creates blockage within the group, within the nation, within humanity. So the key is the individual.

You may have some personal experiences. When you speak ill of someone and you cannot look into his eyes, there is a psychic blockage between you. When there is psychic blockage, the energy of life is not circulating from one life form to another, or from one cell to another. When your energy does not flow and pass into another life form, it stops and accumulates within your form. First it creates whirlpools, then congestions, and then short circuits. These are the names of those causes that create innumerable disorders in our whole system.

When energy circulates you receive nourishment, and you nourish others. It is very interesting that unless energy passes through you, it does not nourish you.

So purification is standing firmly—living, moving, inhaling, and expressing within the energy of the Divine Presence. When the Divine Presence begins to circulate within you, you no longer think in terms of separateness.

The leaders of nations advise us for the sake of business and prosperity to build our nests among the branches of a big tree, but already the roots of that big tree are eaten by gophers. The fall of the tree is a matter of time, but we eat and drink and are merry with each other, opening new businesses, buying new houses, and building new territories. All this is taking place on the tree, but as time goes on the gophers are finishing their job. The gophers are those agents that cut the energy flow from circulation.

Purification is attunement and fusion with Divine Love, or the life-giving essence of creation. Once you are attuned with it, you are not only intelligent but you have insight. You are not only healthy but a source of healing energy, a source of inspiration. You are not only successful, but you make others successful. You are not only a builder, but you are a creative force in the Universe.

It is love that helps you understand, see reality, and be

clear-minded, healthy, joyful, and radioactive. Every kind of separatism and blockage is against our own interests, is against Life.

I remember one day we were making extensive electrical installations in a village for every imaginable use. Money and labor were spent. We lived in the village for ten days far away from our homes. When we finished the job, someone told us that the generator of electricity, which was ten miles away, was blown out by dynamite—and there was no possibility to restore it because it was now a war zone. This is how humanity builds: without consulting the most essential, and wasting its labor.

The path trodden by the server is a life based on Goodness, Beauty, and Truth. Whenever you are living in Goodness, Beauty, and Truth, you are on the Path.

The Path is formed by acts, feelings, and thoughts of

> Goodness
>
> Beauty
>
> Truth

Whoever you are, whatever you are, no matter what religion, political affiliation, race, color, or sex, if you are expressing in your motives and living Goodness, Beauty, and Truth you are on the Path. The Path is the unfoldment, development, and progressive expansion toward the source of Goodness, Beauty, and Truth.

The first definition of the Path is progressive improvement. As we improve, we get closer to our Divine Self, which is a source of Beauty, Goodness, and Truth. There is no improvement except through Beauty, Goodness, and Truth. These are the three colors which lead into the ancient temples of mysteries where revelation is given to the Initiate.

As you manifest Goodness, Beauty, and Truth, you change into Goodness, Beauty, and Truth and you become the Path itself.

When you are trying to live a life of Beauty, Goodness, and Truth, you pass through a great process of purification of fire. The fire we are referring to here is the fire of your Inner Divinity, which burns all that cannot continue to exist in the flame of fire.

It is most difficult to be continuously Beautiful, Good, and True in all our motives and thoughts, emotions, and actions. As we try to stand in Beauty, Goodness, and Truth, we focus the fire of the spirit on our personality and go through a process of burning in which all dross is eventually burned and eliminated. The fire is the Presence of your Divine Self. As you increase in Self-realization, your fire increases, and eventually nothing remains but the Self in the Central Fire. The burning ground is the level where matter and fire meet, where hindrances, obstacles, and limitations meet.

The personality searches for pleasure and comfort, but the developing human soul, once contacting the Inner Guide, no longer is trapped by pleasure and comfort. Curiously enough, the developing human soul lives a life in which most of the time pleasure and comfort are not present, because he knows that *Sattva* binds by pleasure and comfort.

An unfolding human soul eventually realizes that if he pursues a life of pleasure and comfort, he will sooner or later be greedy, materialistic, separative, will deprive people, or will exploit them to a certain degree without being conscious of his acts.

Disciples try to have pleasure and comfort when they are in the outer court, but when they enter into the field of labor of Hierarchy and Shamballa, their comfort and pleasure become sacrificial service for others.

It is very interesting to note that the Great Ones became Greater Ones because they rejected comfort and pleasure for the labor of salvaging humanity.

What will a man expect if he decides to be a Great One?

Let us say ten people are comfortably enjoying themselves in certain pleasures, and then they are invited to leave their comfort and pleasure to rescue the lives of a few people.

Who is going to do such a job? Only those who are already on the path of greatness because such a labor will develop, unfold, purify, organize, uplift and transform them, and make them creative.

Comfort and pleasure are for souls who are identified with their physical, emotional, and mental vehicles and their various conditions. When a man raises himself above the personality, he no longer needs comfort and pleasure because he now has the joy of service and the comfort of sacrifice.

The soul does not need any personality comfort because he realizes that he is immortal, everlasting, limitless, and infinite in his Essence. In front of such a realization, the comfort and pleasure of the personality appear to him as childish games.

Nature does not like anything that is against her nature. That is why Nature has earthquakes, floods, fires, winds, natural catastrophes, and death. Anything done against Nature creates reactions. Reactions are the process of cleaning abnormal things from the system.

Nature does not like you to be sick and die. But it allows you to die, so that next time you act better and do not work against Nature. She tries to give you a new chance with a better body to act in closer harmony with Nature. So Nature tries to correct us and to bring us into harmony with the Divine Law. We reject harmony and act against the Law through acts against Beauty, Goodness, and Truth.

People think that God judges us. God never judges. It is we who judge ourselves; our deeds judge us. If you make a mathematical mistake in your calculation, it is your mistake and you can correct it if you want. The same thing is true of all our mistakes when they make their existence felt through pain and suffering. It is we who judge ourselves, and it is our deeds that judge us, not the Almighty One.

We made Him a judge in our man-made scriptures. When you listen to Christ, He said, "Do not judge others," and He also added, "I, too, did not come to judge you. . . ."

If we, after knowing what we did, do not judge ourselves in the right way, it marks our account for another debt to be paid. We must learn to judge ourselves in the most righteous way. When I am talking about judging ourselves, I am not referring to punishing either body or mind. Judgment is not a matter of punishment but a matter of seeing things as they were, are, and will be.

Real judgment creates an endeavor to correct things that you did wrong, to pay your debts. We bring natural calamities on ourselves because of our transgressions against the laws of Nature. These are not punishments from God; they are reactions to wrong deeds. For example, you play with an electrical wire and burn yourself. Nature did not do that; you did it to yourself.

Nature does not like anything that distorts her harmonious unfoldment, and if anybody tries to break harmony, she causes violent reactions from the disturbed laws.

The Psyche and Psychism, pp. 223-230.

IV

The Great Invocation

The Great Invocation is essentially a prayer which synthesizes the highest desire, aspiration, and spiritual demand of the very soul of humanity.

> *No one can use this Invocation or prayer for illumination and for love without causing powerful changes in his own attitudes; his life intention, character and goals will be changed and his life will be altered and made spiritually useful.*[1]

In New York in 1945, at the time of the June full moon, *The Great Invocation* was given to us. It has become a world Invocation or prayer over these last five decades and has been translated into more than one hundred and forty languages; it is broadcast every day over many radio stations and is used in churches and brotherhoods in nearly all countries. Thousands of people have written about this wonderful Invocation. It has also been made available to the deaf and the blind.

People have expressed a sincere acceptance of the Invocation because it contains an urgent message to all humanity: the human heart is sensitive to sublime beauties, and the world is in need of true guidance and leadership.

Throughout the centuries, many forms of prayer, ritual,

---

[1] Bailey, Alice A., *Discipleship in the New Age II*, p. 168.

and invocation have been given to humanity. They have inflamed the emotions and thoughts of mankind and have led us toward horizons of true survival, toward higher visions of divine achievement. In a sense, they have formed a blueprint to be constructed, a goal to be attained, a task to be fulfilled.

First of all, prayer and invocation attract the aspiration, vision, and hope of the best minds of the race. Secondly, they penetrate into the mind and heart of the masses, creating new response, awakening, and determination. Thus, mankind slowly advances higher and higher upon the path of unfoldment.

As an example, let us take an invocation which was given to us in a different era:

> *O Thou Who givest sustenance to the Universe,*
> *From Whom all things proceed,*
> *To Whom all things return,*
> *Unveil to us the face of the true spiritual Sun,*
> *Hidden in a disc of golden light,*
> *That we may know the truth*
> *And do our whole duty*
> *As we journey to Thy Sacred Feet.*

We can imagine how great the effect of this invocation was on the people who used it in their meditation and vocal aspirations. It is probable that those who used it sincerely created in themselves a new way of thinking, feeling, and acting. It directed their eyes toward That to Which everything returns.

The culture of mankind is the materialized form of all those great aspirations which have been expressed in the human heart and soul throughout centuries, which produced new civilizations and eras. In ancient times, these aspirations and urges were given to humanity by wise men who knew how to direct human emotion and thought through rhythmic prayer, invocation, solemn pledge, and through parables and proverbs.

Prayer and invocation have two degrees of influence. In

the first degree, invocation and prayer have a suggestive influence. It may be group self-suggestion in which the person who uses it releases in himself a new urge toward a better life that surpasses his former self or state of being. In the second degree, it is pure invocation that is directed toward a Great Power about Whom there is no doubt in the user's mind.

Consider the first case. When an invocation or prayer is repeated daily, year after year, with attention and meditation, it produces a real change in man toward betterment. If we recite a prayer or an invocation and meditate upon it, it creates a rhythm in our mental and emotional processes. This rhythmic influence gradually becomes stronger and changes our way of living and acting. That is why we so often repeat our national songs or anthems, vows, different pledges, and mottos. They really affect us and create in us a uniform orientation toward the goal of the invocation.

How much greater is the influence of a pledge or invocation if behind it there is enthusiasm and the recognition of a goal to be achieved. When we truly have faith in the goal expressed in the invocation, when we are able to see the beauty that could be ours by working toward that goal, the rest becomes easy because, sooner or later, strong determination is created in us to achieve that goal in the course of our life.

In the second case, we not only have faith in the goal expressed through the invocation, but we also have faith in that which exists as the Source of creation. When sounding an invocation, we direct our whole being toward that great Existence, evoking response from Him. We direct our "radar" toward space and receive from space rays enriched with a new response. We contact a higher level of consciousness, a new source of inspiration and energy.

Throughout the ages, the dimensions of prayer have gradually shifted to higher levels. In the early ages, masses prayed for the fulfillment of physical and emotional needs.

Prayer then became expressed aspiration for individual enlightenment and love and a request to be led in the right direction. Prayer then emerged from personal limitation and became prayer for the family, group, nation, and eventually for all humanity. Thus, to the degree that the purpose of prayer changed, the wording of prayer also changed; and in relation to these changes, the level and the target of prayer also changed.

In past centuries we asked; we demanded. But in the New Era, we will direct higher energies into the fields of human endeavor. We know that space is an ocean of energy waves in which numerous currents meet, strengthen each other, and transmute or control one another. Mystics of the past used to say that the spark-light produced by a glowworm would exist for eons, floating and expanding in space. They also said that just like the subtler light of the glowworm, every vocal expression continued its existence in space, in some way.

We know that nothing in the Universe is lost; it is only transformed, transmuted into a different form, and expressed again in a different way. If not a single atom is lost, this means that not a single wave of energy is lost. If this is true, then none of our emotional or mental waves are lost; and if they are not lost, they continue their good or bad effects upon human conduct and life.

> *A pure thought ever ascends.*
> *At the feet of Christ it blossoms, radiant.*
> *With pure blue flame glows the Calling Word and radiates the Chalice of Exaltation.*
> *O Lord, drain our tears and perceive the flame of our heart.*
> *By flames shall I dry thy tears and upraise the temple of thy heart.*[2]

---

[2] Agni Yoga Society, *Leaves of Morya's Garden,* Vol. I, para. 21.

When we depart from our loved ones, we use expressions of goodwill, such as, "Have a nice trip," "God be with you," "We wish you success," and so on. With such words, we impart a protective aura or a wave of inspiration and source of sincere joy to them. It is for the same reason that many parents pray for their children and family members to be spared from any danger or temptation, that they may live in the light of their highest dreams and visions. We know many people who pray every morning and night for their loved ones and for humanity as a whole, thus projecting into space a purifying wave of energy—a blessing.

The effect of prayer does not stop here; it is an expanding incense, an illuminating agent, a beam of energy directed toward the Central Power, serving as a channel to that Power. There is an appeal and an answer—invocation and evocation.

When the need is clearly defined, when the fiery aspiration to meet that need is kindled in the heart of the invoking one, then the answer is certain and timely. But to Whom do we appeal? He is the One in Whom we "live, move and have our being." He is the Great Presence, the All-Penetrating Presence.

We live under the illusion that it is only man who is conscious. But man is just an atom, compared to planetary existence. How much smaller he appears if we compare him to a solar system, or to the whole Cosmos. If such an insignificant atom has its own consciousness, isn't it logical to think that atoms smaller than we have consciousness, and conversely, that something larger than we, such as a planet or solar system, has consciousness with which it controls its physical body—a body that is born, lives, grows, and one day dies, just as the human body does? This consciousness guides the activity of that huge body, supporting it and using it in the great Cosmic Plan, just as the human soul uses the human body.

Every cell in our body has its own individual life and consciousness. Collectively, it has body-life and body-consciousness. Isn't this the same relationship that exists between the planet, the solar system, and the individual—who is just an atom or cell when compared to the planet or solar system? If this is true, we can say that there is a Presence Who is everywhere and in everything, in which everything lives, moves, and breathes.

In certain holy sanctuaries, there is a large eye painted above the altar. This is a wonderful symbol, expressing the omnipresence of the Great Existence. But Who is He? The greatest minds in humanity tell us that He is Life. He is the Consciousness that supports and nourishes all and everything.

They also say that everything is Life; everything is materialized, crystallized Life, that Life is everywhere—from the atom to limitless space. Space itself is Life, an ocean of Life—electricity—and this Great Life involves everything.

Throughout the ages, wise ones have told us that this Great Life has three aspects that are present in every atom and cell. Although they are sometimes imprisoned, they are ever ready to be released. There is no lifeless matter or lifeless object. Everything is a part of the Great Life, and it is Life. Everything emerges from that One Life, and returns to the same Life.

We are told that the whole creation is like a figure eight (8). Creation starts from a formless "circle," and begins to materialize through the midpoint, toward the lower "circle," then gradually rises again toward the formless circle.

The Bhagavad Gita expresses this idea very beautifully:

> *All beings were in a state of unmanifestation at their beginning. At the mid-course, they came into manifestation. At the end, they will again enter into the unmanifested state. Then why grieve?*[3]

---

[3] *The Bhagavad Gita* 2:28, translation by Torkom Saraydarian.

Life flows through this great figure eight like an electrical current, materializing and dematerializing continuously—but remaining whole.

We are also told that He is Light, Love, and Will. In other words, He is the Creative Power, the Consciousness of Unity, the Essence of the One Law from Whom radiates all Cosmic, universal, planetary, and social laws in their pure differentiations. He is creativity; He is awareness; He is the Law in every form and in every phenomenon.

Christians say that He is the Father, the Son, and the Holy Spirit—and also one God. There are also people who define Him as positive Cosmic electricity, the negative electricity, and light that emerge when they contact each other.

We are told that this Three-In-One Energy has Its own individual foci, stations, and centers through which It expresses Itself and acts, fulfilling the Will of the Central Life. Each aspect of the Three-In-One Energy has its own centers in extra-planetary, interplanetary, planetary, human, and atomic fields through which it flows, keeping the whole creation alive in a single Will.

The Great Invocation invokes these three energies through all kingdoms of Nature, toward extra-systemic fields where they are centralized with their all-pervading presence. It is the first time in the history of humanity that

a. these three centers are invoked simultaneously by humanity

b. the energies required to meet the planetary needs are so clearly identified

c. all methods are used to make *The Great Invocation* the only aspiration of humanity, everywhere and in every race, "to focus the inchoate mass demand of humanity on to the highest possible level"[4]

---

[4]Bailey, Alice A., *Discipleship in the New Age II*, p. 188.

How to Recite The Great Invocation.

When we repeat a prayer or invocation, we have a tendency to become mechanical after a while. We utter the words and sentences without conscious participation and reap no results.

At the time we say *The Great Invocation,* we must proceed through the following steps:

1. a moment of mental silence
2. a state of penetrative concentration on the meanings of the words
3. the use of creative visualization

Mental silence means detachment from former or new thoughts. *Concentration* means to focus on each word without letting the mind waver, penetrating into the deeper meanings of each word. *Creative visualization* is a process of handling energy and building communication lines to higher levels of being.

All the words that we speak are charged with energy from various levels of our being. If our utterance is mechanical, the words have little power. If we are emotional, they have more power. When we penetrate into the true meaning of our words, they are charged with still more energy. If our consciousness, or being, is focused on higher planes while we speak, our words carry tremendous energy with them, spreading creative effects into space for a very long time.

When we sound an invocation with concentration, visualization, and right tonality, we create a magnetic symphony of colors in space. The Great Law responds with Power, Love, Light, and Beauty. Thus, our needs are fulfilled.

When *The Great Invocation* is intoned by an enlightened group, we have at our disposal the greatest tool to control and handle divine energies in Nature.

Triangles of Fire, pp. 117-126 (Revised edition)

The Great Invocation

*From the point of Light within the Mind of God
Let light stream forth into the minds of men.
Let Light descend on Earth.*

*From the point of Love within the Heart of God
Let love stream forth into the hearts of men.
May Christ return to Earth.*

*From the centre where the Will of God is known
Let purpose guide the little wills of men —
The purpose which the Masters know and serve.*

*From the centre which we call the race of men
Let the Plan of Love and Light work out
And may it seal the door where evil dwells.*

*Let Light and Love and Power
Restore the Plan on Earth.*[5]

---

[5] For a detailed look at *"The Great Invocation"* please see *Triangles of Fire*, by Torkom Saraydarian.

V

The Gayatri

The Gayatri is an invocation, a mantram taken from the *Rig Vedas*. It is prepared in such a way that the successive sounds of the syllables and words produce the right color, vibration, and frequency to create an etheric pipeline between man and the powers he invokes.

The Gayatri is a scientifically composed mantram that is very, very old. For many ages, in many places, Great Ones have used this mantram for the purpose of enlightenment. Enlightenment takes place through seven stages of expansion of consciousness and awareness.

The first enlightenment is called *personality enlightenment,* where you feel that you are in contact with a great reality within yourself. This awareness charges your physical, emotional, and mental vehicles to such a degree that a purification process takes place within those vehicles. The fire of reality causes integration in the vehicles and purifies them to make them receptive to inner guidance.

The second enlightenment is called *Soul enlightenment.* The human soul, the human awareness unit, contacts the Inner Guide and suddenly feels that he is the Self. The Light of the

Solar Angel reveals this mystery in the human soul. The man feels that he is no longer a personality but a living Self. This is a resurrection from the physical, emotional, and mental vehicles and an entrance into the reality of the Self. Thus the real man pulls himself out from his identifications with the personality vehicles and stands in his own reality. Such a man radiates beauty in all of his actions.

The third enlightenment, which is greater than the previously mentioned two, is called *spiritual enlightenment*. At this stage, man comes into contact with the innermost center within himself, the Monad, the Core of his Self. This contact releases a great stream of the energies of Light, Love, and Power from the Spiritual Triad, and this energy radiates out from his physical, emotional, and mental natures; he does not identify with anything that belongs to the not-self, and he does not depend on any outer support or help. The Self is the fountainhead of all that his life needs. Through such an attainment, the purpose and the plan of greater centers radiate out through the man.

The fourth enlightenment is *planetary enlightenment*, when our consciousness embraces all the kingdoms of Nature.

The fifth enlightenment is *solar enlightenment*, when our awareness comes into contact with each center in the solar system.

The sixth enlightenment is the one through which the galactic Plan and Purpose are revealed to us.

At the seventh enlightenment we are free in Cosmic space, like birds that are released from their cages.

The Gayatri is an invocation for enlightenment. People often think that enlightenment comes to them as the lightning strikes the earth. This may be true, but to prepare the conditions for "lightning" sometimes takes ages of strenuous labor.

We are told that this mantram was given to humanity so that it could focus on the fact of enlightenment.

The Psyche and Psychism, pp. 849-850.

> *Above the stratum of earthly thoughts stream the currents of the sun's wisdom, and in these regions begins the great preordained Teaching. We summon to the encompassment of the Universe. But only the instrument of consciousness will permit the new experiments of the blending of spirit and matter.*[1]

In Sanskrit, *The Gayatri* reads:

> *OM*
> *Bhur Bhuva Svah*
> *Tat Savitur Varenyam*
> *Bhargo devasya dhimahi*
> *Dhiyo yonah prachodayat*

A literal translation is:

> *OM*
> *Earth, Mid-world, Heaven,*
> *That life-sun's adorable*
> *Light, God's, let us meditate,*
> *Souls, may enlighten us.*

The free translation may read:

> *OM*
> *All of you who are on earth,*
> *Mid-world, and Heaven,*
> *Let us meditate*
> *Upon the Light adorable*
> *Of the divine Sun of Life*
> *To enlighten our souls.*

---

[1] Agni Yoga Society, *Leaves of Morya's Garden,* Vol. II, "Illumination," p. 43.

In Sanskrit, the word *"Gayatri"* means "to sing out, or protect." It is very interesting to realize that *The Gayatri* is a call to all beings found on both the objective and subjective planes to meditate every day at sunrise and sunset upon the Central Spiritual Sun of the Solar Life and the Monad in each human being. The only refuge for a man is his innermost Self. Once a man achieves such a realization his life sings of beauty, grace, wisdom, love, peace, and bliss.

The Central Spiritual Sun is the source of the true Teaching, the light which penetrates into the three worlds of human endeavor, namely, the physical, emotional, and mental, and into the three planes or worlds of the Universe, namely the physical world, astral world, and mental world. As this supreme Light descends into darker regions of manifestation, it fades out.

The invocation of *The Gayatri* tunes us in with this essence of Light in the three worlds and, as the consciousness of man becomes open to the Light through meditation, the Light increases, human consciousness expands, and eventually enlightenment is achieved.

The three worlds to which *The Gayatri* refers are the lower vehicles of the Central Spiritual Sun within which live entities with corresponding bodies. *The Gayatri* invokes these entities to be ready for a group meditation upon the source of their beauty, the Sun of Life, the supreme Light. In such meditation it will be possible to reach the Source and draw the Light down to the three worlds, establishing therein the paths of Light as guides for all our activities on these three planes.

Five Great Mantrams of the New-Age, pp. 36-37.

The Gayatri is directed to the Central Spiritual Sun. The Sun for us is the powerhouse of heat, light, energy, vitality—even life. But the Sun is the powerhouse of wisdom.

The Sun is the body of an invisible Entity Who sacrifices His body to nourish planets and billions of life-forms in space. It is sometimes called the Great Sacrifice. The Sun not only nourishes physical living forms but also various numberless entities who exist on different planes and spheres, some of which are ahead of us in their evolution, some of which are below us.

The Central Spiritual Sun not only exists in space but also within each atom, animal, human, and superhuman being.

The Sun is triple. We have the visible Sun, the Heart of the Sun, and the Central Spiritual Sun. Our personality comes in contact with the Sun and receives enlightenment. Our soul comes in contact with the Heart of the Sun and receives greater enlightenment: Love-Wisdom. Our innermost Self, the Spirit, comes in contact with the Central Spiritual Sun and is bestowed with power. It is this Central Sun that draws to Himself all sparks scattered throughout the Universe, calling them back through progressive enlightenment.

Enlightenment creates magnetism. Those who are enlightened to a certain degree draw other human beings to enlighten them.

When groups are enlightened, they draw each other and cooperate with each other. When nations are enlightened, they fuse with each other, forming a greater center of light. When humanity is enlightened, it will be one humanity without boundaries and problems of separation.

When humanity is enlightened, it will progress closer to the Hierarchy. When humanity and the Hierarchy are both enlightened, they will come closer to the great Center called the Father's Home. Thus on every step of life, every form of life proceeds along the path of enlightenment.

The Gayatri indicates that occasionally each human being feels in his heart the Light, Love, and Power of the Central Spiritual Sun. Such a feeling reveals to him the path, the purpose, the goal, the destination, and he directs his steps toward the Sun.

When you sunbathe, not only feel the rays of the Sun touching your body, but also feel them penetrating into your emotional nature, enlightening each astral atom, then penetrating into your mental body, enlightening each mental atom. To "enlighten" means to release the hidden spark within each atom.

The Psyche and Psychism, pp. 851-852.

The principle ideas in *The Gayatri* are
    a. synchronous meditation with other beings
    b. existence of the Sun of Life
    c. illumination or enlightenment of our souls

We can also divide the mantram into three parts:

Part One: OM
                Bhur Bhuva Svah

Part Two: Tat Savitur Varenyam
                Bhargo devasya dhimahi

Part Three: Dhiyo yonah prachodayat

Part One harmonizes the vehicles; Part Two causes aspiration, upliftment, and focus; Part Three opens the pathway toward the Sun and invites us to surrender and fuse ourselves with the innermost Light.

Part One refers not only to the physical, astral, and mental worlds but also to the etheric body, the emotional body, and the mental vehicle of man. These three vehicles are harmonized and brought into alignment with the three worlds in the first part of *The Gayatri*.

Analysis of The Gayatri

OM

As we sound the OM, we centralize ourselves within the most sacred Core of our being and enter into deep silence, opening our hearts like a lotus to Cosmic inspiration and bliss. Pantanjali says, "In repeating the OM, and constantly meditating upon it, the obstacles are removed and the consciousness turns inward."[2]

Bhur Bhuva Svah

or

All of you who are on Earth,
Mid-world, and Heaven

Tradition tells us that the sound of these Sanskrit words has the power to harmonize, align, and integrate the three vehicles of man with the three worlds. This power is called *Mantra Shakti*, or energy emanating from words and sounds. Further, these three words refer to the three Deities ruling over these three spheres: Agni, Vayu, and Aditya and Their energies—Will, Love, and Light. In the *Upanishads* we read that the essence of the *Vedas* is also referred to by these three words: *Bhur, Bhuva, Svah*, which originate in the OM and have their existence in OM, which stands as the jewel in the Lotus, or as the developing, unfolding human soul or Self.

These three words are an invitation to all beings living on Earth; whether or not they hear the call, it penetrates into their being and eventually evokes responses in those who are on the path of progress. These words, when uttered with deepest compassion and with a great sense of synthesis, subjectively call all men to their highest duty.

In addition to those who are living on Earth, there are beings who live in the Mid-world. This term refers to the astral

---

[2]*Yoga Sutras of Pantanjali*, I. 29.

plane on which dwell those who have left their bodies or are in the process of reincarnating and are closely related to the objective world. These beings are sensitive to our feelings, imaginations, and love. Since the astral plane is the plane of glamor, this invitation brings a great release to the inhabitants of the Mid-world. They need to be oriented into the light and liberated from their fantasies, glamors, and dreams out of which the atmosphere of the astral plane is formed.

This call, when properly given with concentration and heartfelt sincerity, reaches the inhabitants of the astral plane and urges them to unite in meditation with the being from whom the call emanates. This is of tremendous assistance to those souls who, though caught on the astral plane, are striving to work out their own liberation.

Light emanating from the being sending the call of meditation will guide souls on the astral plane out of the dreams and glamors of that plane. This light, radiated at the time of deep meditation, serves as a torch to lead the dwellers of the astral plane out of darkness and into the light of reality.

Heaven refers to the sphere of the mental plane inhabited by those who have graduated from the astral plane. But this plane may also be a trap because of the great joy, freedom, and bliss found within its sphere. Many souls are content to remain there longer than is necessary and hesitate to return to Earth to work out their past karma through service, labor, and suffering, thereby furthering their own evolution.

The call that goes to the beings on the mental plane, inviting them to come and meditate, may be likened to the ringing of a great bell which invites people to enter the sanctuary of meditation. The call cannot fail to reach those who are in any way associated with us, physically, emotionally, or mentally, whether they are on the objective plane or the subjective plane.

> *Tat Savitur Varenyam*
> *Bhargo devasya dhimahi*

or

> *Let us meditate*
> *Upon the Light adorable*
> *Of the divine Sun of Life*

The object of such a call is to meditate. To meditate means to see the truth and to become the truth. To meditate means to reach deeper into the field of reality and to become a reality.

The divine Sun is the Central Spiritual Sun, the True Self of the solar system from which are emitted those rays of wisdom and energy which lead us back to our Source, the Sun of Life.

According to esoteric wisdom, there is the physical Sun which is the light of the solar system. Then there is the Heart of the Sun from which radiate electromagnetic energies of attraction and love. There is also the Central Spiritual Sun, which is as the Monad—the true spiritual Core of the system and from which emanates the principle of life.

> *Dhiyo yonah prachodayat*

or

> *To enlighten our souls*

is the conclusion of *The Gayatri* and the goal of meditation. In the original Sanskrit, the word "dhiyo" refers to our discriminative faculty which, in a sense, is the human soul.

Enlightenment of the human soul is a gradual process. Meditation upon the Inner Sun builds the channel through which Light descends into the human soul, whereby man is enabled to discriminate between the Real and the unreal.

The first great enlightenment occurs when, through meditation, the intuitional Light illumines the entire sphere of the mental plane and man takes the first higher initiation—the Transfiguration—in which he comes to realize that his identity is one with the Central Spiritual Sun. This Light enters the mind gradually, as a result of the service and meditation of the individual, and leads him into illumination and realization. Man cannot live according to the principles he teaches nor according to the laws he accepts unless the Light of Intuition penetrates his mental atmosphere. When this occurs his agelong identification with his lower bodies and their inertia, glamor, and illusions drops away and he sees himself "face to face."

A beautiful verse referring to the Light is found in *Yajnavalkya Samita,* which reads:

> *The spiritual light which is hidden within the Sun is the light adorable. It shines through the hearts of all creatures as their consciousness.*
>
> *The spiritual light which shines through the physical sun shines through the hearts of every human soul.*
>
> *The light which shines in the heart of all human souls in the form of consciousness shines also through the universe which, as a heavenly man, is a living organism.*

In the *Isavas Upanishad* 15, we find:

> *O Lord, You nourish and sustain all that exists. Please remove the disk of the shining sun, so that as I travel on the Path, I can see Your Face behind the Veil of the Sun.*

In esoteric books we are told that the physical Sun provides fire by friction, the Heart of the Sun gives us solar fire, and from the Central Spiritual Sun comes the spiritual-electrical fire. *The Gayatri* not only focuses our attention and consciousness upon the Central Spiritual Sun, from which emanate life currents, but also invites us to focus, through meditation, upon the Central Core, the True Self within us, within each being. This is the true "North" by which all the directions of our life's ship are controlled. Those who meditate and gradually come closer to this Central Self will find that their physical problems will be dissolved, their glamors, daydreams, and illusions will be eliminated, and they will start on the pure Path of the divine Sun. They will follow this path in the light of their spiritual Self and gradually become detached from their pseudo-selves, egos, urges and drives, and stand in the light of their true destination.

As a result of this enlightenment, the spiritual evolution of the meditators progresses and they take their next step on the path of reality. Those who dwell on the astral plane move forward and those who are enchanted in the heavenly world proceed to the path of duty and responsibility on the physical or other planes.

This group meditation, entered into in conjunction with beings either in or out of the physical body, accomplishes a great upsurge toward the Sun, sheds light into the human soul, and challenges the meditator to advance toward his Cosmic destiny.

Some people believe that the repetition of *The Gayatri* by itself brings results. This is not so. It is the repetition of this mantram combined with meditation upon the Central Spiritual Sun that releases man from his agelong prison and admits him on the path of his divine heritage.

The Gayatri is a seed-thought for advanced disciples and initiates who, after a long life of meditation and service, eventually reach the realization that the manifested Universe is the expression of the Central Spiritual Sun, which is the True Self of the Universe. Gradually, all their meditations focus upon the supreme seed-thought—the Central Spiritual Sun in the Universe and in man. They may meditate upon any subject, as long as it is a part of the expression of the Central Spiritual Sun, the Self.

Through such meditation, man will gradually contact his Inner Core and begin to live and express himself as that Core, the Self.

Five Great Mantrams of the New-Age, pp. 37-42.

A Visualization

1. In meditation visualize the Central Sun. See each of Its rays coming and forming a center of light within you, which is your True Self. Your True Self is an extension of the Central Spiritual Sun.
2. Visualize that the light within you is increasing and eventually radiating out through your mental, emotional, and physical vehicles, purifying and enlightening them.
3. Visualize that the Self within you is one with the almighty Spiritual Sun. Then radiate this awareness toward humanity, toward all life, so that it gradually creates the one symphony of Life.
4. Visualize living beings from various places on Earth and the astral and mental planes sitting around you doing the same meditation. You can even mentally say to them, "Let us sit together in a synchronous and unanimous meditation, and direct all of our being to the Central Spiritual Sun."
5. Visualize the light within you and within the others increasing, building a bridge between your Core and the Core of the Universe.

These entities factually exist. They wait for you to call them to meditate with you. They increase the light of your astral and mental bodies, while you increase their light on whatever level they are found. In this way you form a group, a center to invoke and evoke light.

On the astral plane there are millions of entities who need light and guidance. Suspended on the etheric planes, there are millions of entities who are striving for light. They are those who used heavy drugs, committed crimes, or committed suicide. They are in their etheric bodies, and your light may lead them to proceed on their way toward the mental plane to reincarnate on the physical plane.

In the astral plane there are glamored people whose astral bodies are crystallized. These are mostly greedy people, people who indulged in excessive pleasure, people who are attached to earthly interests and desires. Some of them are hatha yogis who crystallized their astral bodies to such a degree that they cannot shed them. Your light helps them.

The Psyche and Psychism, pp. 852-853.

The Gayatri is divided into three parts:
1. All of you who are on Earth, Mid-world, and Heaven
2. Let us meditate upon the light adorable of the divine Sun of Life
3. To enlighten our souls

Part One stands for the synchronization of the physical, emotional, and mental bodies with the physical, astral, and mental worlds and with their inhabitants. With the first part you are sending your invitation and call to those who aspire to be in group meditation on these planes. It often happens that if you miss your appointed time of meditation, those who have regularly joined you will awaken you or remind you to do your meditation. Thus you create friendship between yourself and those who are

- in physical bodies, but come and join your meditation with their subtle bodies
- in the astral plane and need mental guidance to proceed on their way to higher planes
- in the mental plane and want to inspire you or receive inspiration to further the enlightenment of their souls

The inhabitants of these planes who share in your meditation can be human souls, devas, or angels.

Through your early morning meditation, you share the light that your friends absorb, or they share your light and carry it to those who are associated with them. Thus meditation eventually turns into a festival of light.

Through meditation, we nourish those who are thirsty for Light, Love, and Energy, and thus become a subjective server to many souls. The radiance of meditation penetrates into many dark spheres and sheds light there. Eventually, your meditation becomes an Ashram, a classroom in which you give or receive instruction.

The supreme obligation of every soul is to establish conscious contact with the Central Spiritual Sun.

While repeating The Gayatri, the following practical steps should be taken:

1. Sit calmly, detached, and in deep joy.
2. Concentrate your consciousness as high as possible, to the mental plane or Intuitional Plane.
3. Keep silent in that high-point of achievement.
4. Visualize sparks of light—souls—from physical, emotional, and mental planes, sitting around you in circular formation, all ready to meditate.
5. Sound *The Gayatri* very slowly, understanding each word and without letting your mind falter. As you sound it, visualize the spark-souls and also the Central Sun. See

rays emanating from the Sun, touching every spark and making them shine out in great light until you see the whole group as a unified field of light.

6. Start thinking about the Sun within yourself and your relation to it.
7. Let your soul be enlightened with all the other souls, radiating out fragrance and multicolored rays. You may visualize your soul as a drop of light, from the center of which a beam of light extends and penetrates into the Sun.
8. Visualize a stream of light from the Sun traveling through the beam of light toward the drop of light.
9. See the drop of light expand, turning into an ocean of light which purifies and heals all of your personality vehicles and sanctifies your entire environment. A great healing process can take place at this time if you are geared to the Light.
10. See the Sun pouring light all over the world. Repeat:

     Let Light stream forth into the minds of men.
     Let Light descend on Earth.
11. Slowly feel your body and environment.
12. Open your eyes and rest for a few minutes.

With joy, engage yourself thereafter in your daily duties and responsibilities. You can do this meditation for fifteen minutes, once a week.

When you repeat *The Gayatri*, especially in its Sanskrit form, you create a tremendous, unique vibration, a protective shield around you through which no low-level or hostile vibrations can reach you. You build this shield every time you repeat *The Gayatri* with great solemnity and joy.

Also, as you invoke more light, it is important not to act against light in your daily life. Invoking greater light may create major problems in your nature if you resist light and hinder it with your actions, words, and thoughts. One cannot invoke light and then fight against it without consequences.

The Gayatri is a protective mantram because it unifies you with the Source. It is only in unity that fear disappears and safety is built.

The Psyche and Psychism, pp. 855-857.

VI

The Lord's Prayer

In these times, some people think that prayer is old-fashioned, or out of fashion, but it is not. Those who think so deprive themselves from higher sources, higher energies, higher guidance. Some people depend only on themselves and say, "We are going to heal ourselves," while others pray for healing. Those who pray for healing and in the meantime do whatever is necessary to heal themselves have a greater opportunity and chance to be healed, because they are using resources that are not available to a human being unless he prays.

What does prayer do? Prayer connects the human being to the resources that are invisible that can really affect his life, guide, protect, and lead him. Why deny such a Source? I personally know of many instances where prayer cured people who were considered to be incurable by medical professionals. **Prayer cured them.** Prayer also helps people solve many problems or escape from danger.

Someone once called before one of our meetings, saying, "My son has had an accident and is paralyzed. There is no hope that he will survive. Will you pray for him?" There were about eighty of us at the meeting, and we prayed for him. In closing the prayer, we said, "Thy Will be done." After I returned home, the boy's parents called me and said, "The doctors said a miracle happened. Our son is recovering. One of the doctors said, 'Within medical knowledge, this is an impossibility because the spine is severely damaged and the nerves are severed.'"

A lady once came to me before a meeting and said, "My granddaughter has been lost for two days. Can you ask the group to pray for her after the lecture?" After the lecture, I asked the group to visualize the sixteen-year-old girl walking in darkness with an Angel holding her hand, bringing her home. "Please pray for the Lord to send His Angel to her," I requested. The next morning, the grandmother came to me and said, "She has returned home! She had left to go with a man to the mountains, but she suddenly felt that she must return home. She left him and ran back." She verified that her granddaughter decided to return at the same time the group was praying for her assistance. We can believe in prayer.

When you pray, not only do you secure the assistance of higher forces but you create courage, daring, inspiration, fearlessness, and the power to fight against hindrances and restrictions within yourself. It is psychological, spiritual, and scientific. Knowing all of these things, Christ wanted to teach humanity how to pray, so He gave us the most beautiful prayer. After giving that prayer, He wanted His disciples to learn it by heart and spread it everywhere. He also wanted them to think and meditate upon it and make that prayer a seed thought and a plan for their lives. The Lord's Prayer is a very powerful prayer, and there are so many deeper meanings behind the words.

It begins, *Our Father Who art in heaven.* This is a very simple phrase, but it is the cornerstone for human survival. If people only realized the meaning of this phrase, cultures and civilizations of the world would change.

Our Father acknowledges that we have one Father—one Source. We are all children of the Most High. This means that we must not slander our brothers and sisters. We must not slander and butcher them; we must not steal from them. Instead, we must take care of them because they are our brothers and sisters. If we do not take care of our brothers and sisters, we slander our Father. This is a very important point. When a father sees his children killing each other, how does he feel?

Christ gave this strong seed thought, which strongly impressed the disciples' brains. He said, "Pray just like this. Say, 'Our Father, Who art in heaven.'" Are you acting in a way that you understand the Fatherhood of God? If you do, you will never destroy other nations with bombs or genocide. You will really realize that we all are the children of one Father.

A new civilization can be constructed upon this one phrase—*Our Father Who art in heaven*. Human beings do not see each other as brothers and sisters, but as enemies or competitors. They are afraid of each other. But see how Christ gave this beautiful vision for humanity? Of course, in other religions this idea has been cultivated in different forms and expressions. But Christ brought it into focus so that humanity could experience it, feel it and know it. We all have a father and brothers and sisters, so this kind of relationship is something we can really understand.

Something else is revealed in this sentence. If our Father created everything, then animals, fish, birds, and trees are also our little brothers and sisters. Christ gave us a philosophy that cannot be surpassed. No one in the world has said, "Our Father, we are all Your children."

The Great Sage says that the highest Teaching was given by Christ. We do not need a lot of philosophy or psychology—just the realization of this prayer.

It is important to say this prayer without being mechanical. We must ponder it and go deeper into it, asking ourselves, "Did I insult or slander You, my Father? Did I slander your children?" How sensitive we become when we do this. How harmless, how caring we become when we realize that we all have the same Father. We cannot slander, criticize, or kill each other because our Father is watching us. He loves all of His children, regardless of their color or how obnoxious they act. The Father forgives them because He is present in each of them. This statement contains a very strong charge of energy. In each human being the Father is present, just as your physical father is present within you.

Scientists are now conducting research to discover what the gene is. If you really think about it, the gene is your father and mother existing within you. Spiritually, God exists within you; God is your root. But we hate and massacre each other in the name of God. We think that whatever we know is the "absolute truth," and that beyond this nothing exists. This is a great hallucination.

We know one thing: our knowledge, our abilities and powers are limited to our current stage of evolution. Beyond this, greater evolutions exist. Those who penetrate into the Fatherhood of God will never condemn, slander, or kill each other, or limit the expanding consciousness of their brothers and sisters.

The Lord's Prayer is formulated on seven levels. The first level is an invocation: *Our Father Who art in heaven.* What does *heaven* mean? A president visiting here from another country said, "We are sending rockets and equipment into space, but we have not met anyone in heaven yet." His words are an expression of his ignorance. "Heaven" actually means space—the whole space. "Heaven" means limitless space, whether with or without form. **Space is God.** Is space limited? If so, how are we going to reach that limit? By traveling for five million years? How many millions of times are we going to be born and die in a spacecraft to reach the limits of space? God is limitless! With this prayer, we invoke that Great

Presence Who is everywhere, in everything, and Who also dwells within us.

Hallowed be Thy Name. What does "hallowed" mean? "Hallowed" means health and wholeness. In saying "hallowed," we are saying, "Your Name, Your Presence, Your Existence must be one in all of our minds, hearts, and being." Consciously we must realize that He exists within us as One Entity. If we realize this, we can create a super-culture and a super-civilization, not a civilization that is condemned to death. What kind of civilization is it that pollutes the water and then drinks it? What kind of civilization pollutes the air and then inhales the poison? What kind of civilization poisons the vegetable kingdom and then eats from it? Can you imagine such an insane civilization? This is what humanity is, especially its scientists.

Hallowed be Thy Name also says, "Your Name is so adored by me; I give the highest respect to Your Name. I know Your Name is within me. I know Your Name is within everyone. I know Your Name is one within everything." What is the Name? It is His Glory, His Light. It is He. **His Presence is always manifested with Light.**

There are some very interesting ideas about the word "name." If you study the *New Testament,* you will see that every human being has three names: a name as a personality; as a soul; and a name for the Monad, the Self, the pure Divine Self. When you are baptized in the Christian church, you are given a name as a personality. For example, you are named Jesus. At the Third Initiation, you are given another name in a dream or through your initiation. They say, "You are Christ now." Then at the Fifth Initiation, you receive another name; They say, "You are Jesus Christ, our Lord—Light, Love, and Power."

The same thing happens to us. We have a name; then we receive another name when we take the Third Initiation. When we take the Fifth Initiation, another name is given to us.

Names are indications of the level of consciousness on

which a person functions, his level of beingness. Every time our beingness changes, our consciousness changes and we have a different name. For example, a person is a sergeant; then he becomes a colonel, then a general. He is the same person, but because he is functioning with different mechanisms on different planes, with different responsibilities and duties, his name changes. **His name is always related to his level of consciousness, to the Light he has, and to the responsibilities with which he is engaged.**

Thy Kingdom come. This is like saying, "Let Light descend on Earth. May Christ return to Earth." *Thy Kingdom* refers to the activities of Love, to the externalization of the Hierarchy.

We see Light and Love, then, *Thy Will be done*—Power, Will, as in, "Let Light and Love and Power restore the Plan on Earth."

The prayer then continues with four phrases which are related to the "squares." "Squares" are in human beings—etheric, physical, astral, and mental—"human squares."

Give us this day our daily bread, and forgive us our debts, as we forgive our debtors. See how it comes to the human level? One is physical (eating), one is astral, and one is mental.

Next, *Lead us not into temptation, but deliver us from evil* is the same as saying, "And may it seal the door where evil dwells," which is dealing with the etheric level.

The Great Invocation is the Invocation of Christ. Master Tibetan says that two thousand years before Christ was born as a human being on this Earth, He was sounding that Invocation before the Hierarchy. If Christ was sounding this Invocation in the Presence of Hierarchy four thousand years ago, what did He mean by, "May Christ return to Earth"? **Christ is a redemptive, regenerative, saving, illuminating, transforming Presence in the Cosmos. He is a Ray from the Cosmic Christ.**

The next section is called the doxology: *Thine is the Kingdom*—Light, Glory (which is Love), and Power (which is will power). Christ built The Lord's Prayer in such a geometrical way that it always invokes the Father, the Son, and the Holy Spirit. The Holy Spirit is Light; the Father is will power, or Purpose. It is interesting how *The Great Invocation* is built in exactly the same geometrical configuration as the Lord's Prayer, but with different wording.

Actually, before we do anything, we should pray. For example, if you have just started a new job, say the Lord's Prayer, and if you are not too busy, say *The Great Invocation*. By doing this, you expose yourself to those energies and forces that will enlighten and protect you, that will clean away obstacles and difficulties, or give you the courage to clean them. Eventually, prayer will make you a successful Son of God.

When Jesus said, "I am a Son of God," they crucified Him. But in Psalms 82, it is written, "You are Sons of God." What does "Sons of God" mean? It does not mean that God is married and having children. It means that we are emanations from Him. Every ray is a son of the Sun, just like our books, our music, our dances are our children, our sons. Do not take these things literally. Understand them metaphorically, in deeper ways, so that you understand the symbology behind them.

Thy Kingdom come. What is the *Kingdom* that is coming? There are the animal, vegetable, and mineral kingdoms, as well as the human kingdom. We call them kingdoms esoterically because every kingdom has a king, who is a great soul or deva that is the "general manager" of that kingdom. For example, the animal kingdom has a "general manager." In A *Treatise on Cosmic Fire*,[1] the Tibetan Master says a great Avatar is working

---

[1] Bailey, Alice A., Lucis Publishing Company, New York, New York.

with the animal kingdom as His Garden to develop its evolution, to promote animals and eventually graduate them from the animal kingdom. Very soon this Avatar is supposed to appear to protect the animal kingdom.

What will happen if this Avatar takes us to "court?" I wrote about this in *The Unusual Court*. It says, "How many lives, how many cows and oxen have you eaten and why did you do that?" Of course we have the vanity to think that man is the king of Nature, that he can do anything he wants. What a great illusion and deception this is! Mankind is not even the slave of Nature. A king would not destroy his own kingdom! Animals are smart enough to live naturally, but man has created an unnatural life that is destructive to himself.

Thy Kingdom is the next kingdom. When we graduate from the human kingdom, we will be part of the Hierarchy. Our consciousness will live in the Intuitional and Atmic Planes, instead of working in the brain. Is this possible? Of course it is possible! If humanity came from the animal kingdom and became human beings, the human kingdom must also graduate and proceed to a higher level.

Thy Kingdom is "May Christ return to Earth," the externalization of the Hierarchy. Two thousand years ago, He planted this seed in the human brain to make us aware that there is a divine kingdom somewhere and that it must manifest on Earth. The entire book, *The Externalisation of the Hierarchy,*[2] is based on this one sentence: *Thy Kingdom come.*

Thy Will be done on Earth as it is in heaven. All of the suffering, pain, and failure of humanity are because of cleavages in its consciousness and nature. The failure of humanity and the planet is due to these cleavages. With these words, Christ wanted to heal those cleavages. As you think, so you act. *Thy Kingdom come, Thy Will be done on Earth as it is in heaven.*

---

[2]*Ibid.*

For example, you think something right, you feel something, you create something, and then do it. When you follow through, you are whole; you are healthy because you are not divided within yourself. You do not think one way and act another. Instead you think, feel, and act in the same way. You are an integrated, aligned person. This is how a group must be, a church must be, a nation must be and how humanity must be.

Two thousand years ago Christ planted this seed thought so that infant humanity would think about it and change its life. What have we done? We have acted exactly the opposite. We have acted against our own survival. If you study the history of humanity from the time of Christ until now, it is a history of bloodshed. Of course, great cultures came, but they did not change us. Except for a few people who made breakthroughs and entered into higher levels of consciousness, we are the same beasts that we were at that time. Those people who made breakthroughs became part of the *Kingdom*.

What is this *Kingdom?* Is it Christian? Does it belong to any particular religion? No, it is universal; it consists of the children of God who are enlightened, who have conquered life. They are from every race, from every religion, from every nation.

We will be very surprised when we end up sitting next to those whom we hated because of their religion, race, and nationality. Why is this? We have created a myth all over the world by saying, "If you do not belong to our religion, you are going to hell. There is no escape."

Why create such separatism in our consciousness? I have traveled all over the world and I have seen unimaginable things. For example, I was a strong Christian because of my background and because of the first monastery where I studied. When I finally visited Buddhist temples, I met Buddhist monks who were ten thousand years ahead of those I saw in other temples and monasteries. In my mind I thought, "The Kingdom of God should consist only of Buddhists." Then I began studying Sufi mysticism, and met Sufi Teachers Who had oceans of wisdom, power, and beauty. Next I thought that the Kingdom of God was surely Moslem. I then went to Jerusalem to a Jewish university where I met some Rabbis who were so "deep" that I thought that the Kingdom of God must be Jewish. When I returned to the world, I wondered who was going to be in the Kingdom of God. The answer is obvious: all of them!

Those who love and sacrifice are those who are in the Kingdom. The Great Ones eagerly come to us and say, "You silly children; behave and come to your senses because the Father is One and we are all His children." We have heard this idea so many times that it has become commonplace in our minds and speech. If we pause a moment and think deeply about the phrase, *Our Father,* we will see that if it is true (and it cannot be untrue), we came from one Source and are going to return to the same Source.

You are going to change your life. It is a most difficult endeavor to start changing yourself because you must undo whatever you have been doing for millions of years.

There was a Bishop who was greatly esteemed and who held a very high position in the church. One day the church officials said to him, "Your Highness, Your Beatitude, there are three ignorant ascetics living on an island. You must go and teach them from the *Bible* because we must save them." So the Bishop went to the island where they lived, and indeed found that they were very ignorant people. But unknown to the Bishop, their intuition, clairvoyance, and clairaudience were highly operative. He said to them, "My children, you are living in ignorance. How do you pray to God?" They replied in one voice, "God, we are ready to help You." "No," he said to them, "that is wrong. You must say, 'God help us, have pity and mercy on us so that our sins evaporate.'" "Okay," they answered, because he was a Bishop.

For four or five hours the Bishop taught them how to pray. Finally they learned, so he boarded a boat and set out for home. In the meantime, the three ascetics forgot the prayer he had given to them and so they pondered what to do. "We must go after the Bishop in his boat and again ask him how to pray because we have forgotten. He told us we were sinning by not knowing it." So the three ignorant ascetics walked across the surface of the water after the boat. Coming across the waves by foot, they neared the boat, and waving to the Bishop from the water, shouted, "Please tell us the prayer again; we have forgotten it." He looked at them standing on the water and said, "Go back to praying any way you want!"

We are people of formality and fashion. We think, "If you don't pray like me, you are going to hell. If you don't read my books, too bad for you." These attitudes are cosmetics. It is important to believe in your inner beauty, the inner tie with that Almighty Space—the Father. If you are in contact with the Father, you are the most advanced human being, even if you do not have a little piece of paper in your pocket that says you are a Ph.D. When you enter into Higher Worlds, They will not ask what degree of education you have; They will ask, "What did you do for humanity? How much did you forget yourself for the sake of your brothers and sisters?"

Once my Teacher said to me, "When you knock on the door of heaven and ask to enter, They will shout and say, 'Who is there?' If you are really ready to enter, you will know the answer. I can tell you the answer, but you will not fool the Guardians. You will say, 'Nobody.'" "Teacher," I asked, "why say 'nobody'?" "Because," he replied, "you gave of yourself continuously and now nothing remains of you." I told him that I would write a book about this in the future.

It is not a person's education, his position, or possessions that gain his entrance into the Kingdom of God. How much of him is left? If twenty-five percent is still left, he is still in hell twenty-five percent. If nothing remains of him, if he has given all that he is to everyone, he lost his cards but won the game.

"Giving yourself away" means

1. Removing the weights from your shoulders. A few examples of "weight" are vanity, ego, glamor, illusion, hatred, malice, slander, jealousy, revenge, and fear. Cleanse yourself and get rid of these.

2. Giving of your time, energy, and wisdom. Eventually a time will come when you will never think about yourself. You will only think of ways you can help others. Humanity is fifty million years late in its understanding of this. Whatever human beings are doing now is for their own pitiful selves, the group-self, or national-self. This is totally against the Law of the Fatherhood of God.

We have had enough of saying, "Me, me, me, ours, ours, ours." Where has this taken us? We tried this for eighteen million years, but it did not work. A good business person would say, "If I cannot do good business in the old way, let me change my approach and find another way to do it." We are not even good businessmen. We must change.

Armament has never helped bring peace to humanity. Instead, we can destroy the world. Can we think of another solution to save the world? It requires a change of mentality.

Hatred has never worked. Who are you hating? You are hating yourself in other human beings. How can you hate God within another person? It is absurd. If you philosophically delve behind these words, there are tremendous levels which have not yet been discussed.

Our *daily bread*. Some people have translated this to mean

going to the supermarket and buying tomatoes and potatoes, bread, and so on. "Daily bread" is our daily ideas, visions, inspirations, and higher contacts. Christ said, "You do not live by bread alone, but you live by the words of God." This means we live by the Light of God.

The phrase "daily bread" is totally different than our usual interpretation of it. For example, our books are daily bread; our meditation is "chewing" the "bread." In this way we understand what we are reading. "Daily bread" is our daily vision, daily love. Love is our bread; sacrifice is our bread.

Lead us not into temptation. This phrase is not an accurate translation from the Aramaic, but in various translations seen in the United States and Britain, it is translated this way. A more accurate translation reads, *Give us power over temptation.* This is totally different from that to which most people are accustomed.

Why would we ask God not to lead us into temptation, and why would God be eager to lead us into temptation? We are weak if we ask this. On the contrary, we go to school and say, "Give me difficult tests so that I can pass." The sportsman wants greater hindrances to overcome; he says, "Give me power to overcome the temptations or traps, to see the traps and not fall into them." It is good to see the traps. Why would God want to keep you ignorant and say, "The world is paradise; you are going to live in paradise and not know evil."? On the contrary, He says, "You will see what evil is and I will give you the energy, courage, and daring to overcome evil."

The Lord's Prayer is a magnificent building, a magnificent construction of power and plan. We can build our lives upon this prayer, but we have forgotten about it. We ask, "Why pray? Eat, drink, and sleep—that is all there is." But prayer is very important. When a person prays, he finds a way toward Home. If we do not pray, we lose the path leading Home.

You can be the most despicable person, but if you pray, it

is possible to transform yourself. Once my Father was asked, "Which human beings do you like the most?" He answered, "The most rotten ones." That was a great answer because there is hope for everyone. Any person can become a conscious Son of the Almighty One. Essentially you are this Son; you just have to realize it. It is a matter of admitting it and realizing it, nothing else.

Some people think that prayer is an act of channeling. Conscious contact with higher forces is not a form of blind channeling. If a person is consciously having a relationship with a higher force, this is wonderful. But if he does not really know how he is doing this, he places himself in grave danger. There is nothing wrong in these practices except when a person dresses himself as a doctor and performs surgery on someone without knowing what he is doing. This is objectionable.

A medium once said to me, "I am channeling a Great One." I told her she was channeling a dark force because she was giving messages about hatred, malice, slander, jealousy, killing, and so on. I said, "Be careful." If a person is in conscious contact with his purified nature, with higher forces, this is what vision is. He can stand here and be in contact with higher forces that illuminate his mind and send ideas and visions about which he speaks. But such a person consciously knows what he is doing.

Prayer also puts us in touch with our Guardian Angel, but this depends upon what we know, what we are doing, and how sincere and conscious we are about the impressions and inspirations we receive. It also depends upon the condition of our mental and spiritual mechanisms. We are masterpieces; we are universes, but we have not yet developed. When we walk, we must walk between earth and heaven, balancing all of these things.

Christ said, "It is My Father talking through Me. I am not speaking anything but My Father's words." He knew that

Presence was His Father. He was pure enough to stand in that Fire and speak. It is a matter of developing and purifying ourselves and consciously doing the things that we do.

The Father is everywhere and in everything. He is here! He is Omnipresent, the Most High. You cannot even give a name to Him. The Chinese refer to God as *Tao*. If you ask what Tao is, they say, "Something we do not know."

God is known only to the degree which a person is. If the person is, symbolically speaking, a one-degree person, imagine that God[3] is ten billion degrees ahead of him. How can we gradually elevate and expose ourselves to that Light so that, eventually, "Purpose guides the little wills of men"?

See how beautiful the Lord's Prayer is? This evening before going to sleep, say the Lord's Prayer and think about what a complex and beautiful symphony it is.

From *The Lord's Prayer,* Lecture by Torkom Saraydarian,
March 30, 1988

---

[3] See also *One Hundred Name of God.*

Index

A
Animals 62
Armament 66
Aspiration
  and prayer 16
Astral plane
  and guidance 51
  as Mid-world 45
Aura
  and vices 22
Avatar
  and animal kingdom 62

B
Beauty 24
Beauty, power of
  how restored 7
Blockage
  individual to national 22
Blood
  in various bodies 21
Bread
  meaning of 67
Burning ground 25
Business
  and adaptation 66

C
Center, heart 8
Centers
  and impurities 20
Channeling
  dangers of 68
Christ
  and Father's words 69
  and Great Invocation 60
  and Lord's Prayer 63
Civilization, new

  and Lord's Prayer 57
Comfort and pleasure 26
Consciousness
  and name 60
  of atom and cosmos 33
Consciousness, level of
  and devotion 16
  and prayer 14
Courage
  defined 12
Creativity, level of
  and prayer 16
Culture
  defined 30

D
Deities, three 45
Desires
  and prayer 15
Devotion
  and prayer 16
Dhiyo
  defined 47
Disciples
  inner/outer courts 25
Doubt
  and prayer 16
Dreams
  kinds of 11
Drug addiction 20

E
Ego 5
Eight, the number
  as symbol 34
Elephants
  how trapped 8
Emotional purification 19
Energy circulation 23
Energy wave
  existence of 32

Enlightenment
  and magnetism 43
  stages of 39
Entities
  in Subtle Worlds 51
Evil
  and hypocrisy 6
Evocation, law of 14
Eye, large
  as symbol 34

F
Father
  in prayer 57
Fatherhood of God 66
Fire
  and purification 25
Freedom
  defined 11
Future
  and prayer 15

G
Gayatri 39
  and meditation 49
  how to say 52
Gene
  defined 58
Giving yourself
  defined 66
God
  and judgement 26
  how to know 69
Goodness 7, 24
Gophers 23
Great Invocation 29
  and three energies 35
  how to recite 36
Great Ones 25
Groups
  and energy circulation 22

Guardian Angel
  and prayer 68

H
Habits
  as protest 20
Hallowed
  defined 59
Hatred 66
Healing
  and prayer 55
Health
  and relationship to pain 21
Heaven
  as space 58
Hierarchy 62
Higher Worlds
  and sleep 10
  education vs. service 65
Humanity
  failure of 62
Hypocrisy 6

I
Imagination 16
Improvement 24
Impurities in bodies
  actions of 20
Initiate 24
Initiation
  and names 59
Inner Guide 16
  and prayer 15
Intuition 48
Invocation
  results of 30
Invocation, law of 14

J
Joy
  how expressed 9
Judgment 27

K

Kingdom, Gods
  defined 63
Kingdoms
  of nature 61

L

Law of Association 20
Life
  defined 34
Life, direction in 5
Light, Love, Will 35
Lord's Prayer 56
  levels of 58
Love 24

M

Mantra Shakti
  Deities, three 45
Meditate
  defined 47
Meditation 49
Meditation, group 52
Mental purification 19

N

Names
  kinds of 59
National songs
  and anthems 31
Nations
  reason for decline 22
Nature
  reactions of 26

O

OM 45
Orphans 5

P

Pain
  and healing 21
Pain, cause of
  in process of healing 21
Path
  defined 24
Planes, higher 62
Prayer
  and going Home 67
  and inner rejection 15
  Atmic 17
  changes in time 32
  defined 13
  Intuitive 17
  meaning in history 30
  qualities of 55
  result of 61
Prayers
  and answers to 14
  and evolution 14
  interference to 16
Prosperity
  defined 12
Protest
  forms of 20
Prototypes
  contact with 17
Psychic blockage 23
Psychic energy
  and circulation of 22
  circulation of 21
Psychic repair 10
Purification
  and Divine Presence 23
  as painful 19
  elements needed 20

R

Recitation
  of prayers 36
Religious pretention 6
Rhythm of Nature

daily worship 5
Righteousness 8

S
Sattva 25
Self
   and re-creating 17
Self, Divine
   and Path 24
Separatism 24
Service, sacrificial 25
Sleep
   and prayer 10
   how to 11
Son of God
   defined 61
Soul, human
   development of 25
   enlightenment 47
Stories,
   Of prayers/inappropriate requests 14
Story:
   Of Bishop and ascetics/real prayer 64
   Of boy and hashish/wrong desires 15
   Of channeling/being unconscious 68
   Of electricity/ waste of labor 24
   Of entering heaven/give of yourself 65
   Of injured boy/prayer 55
   Of lost girl/prayer 56
   Of various monasteries/ Kingdom of God 63

Sun
   and fires 48
   as body 43
   three parts of 47
Sun, Central Spiritual 52
Sun, Central Spiritual 42
Sun, course of
   and worship 12

T
Tao
   and God 69
Teaching
   source of 42
Temptation
   defined 67
Transfiguration 48
Trinity 35
Truth 24

V
Vanity 5
Vices
   and deterioration 22
Vices, kinds of
   as weights 66
Visualization 17
   on Central Spiritual Sun 50

W
Words, spoken
   how charged 36
Worship 5
   fifth one 10
   first one 6
   fourth one 9
   second one 7
   third one 8
Worship, five-pointed
   results of 6

ABOUT THE AUTHOR

Torkom Saraydarian (1915-1997) was born in Asia Minor. Since childhood he was trained in the Teachings of the Ageless Wisdom.

He visited monasteries, ancient temples, and mystery schools in order to find the answers to his questions about the mystery of man and the Universe.

He lived with Sufis, dervishes, Christian mystics and masters of temple music and dance. His musical training included the violin, piano, oud, cello, and guitar. It took long years of discipline and sacrifice to absorb the Ageless Wisdom from its true sources. Meditation became a part of his daily life, and service a natural expression of his soul.

Torkom Saraydarian dedicated his entire life to the service of his fellow man. His writings and lectures and music show his total devotion to the higher principles, values, and laws that are present in all world religions and philosophies. These works represent a synthesis of the best and most beautiful in the sacred culture of the world. His works enrich the foundational thinking on which man can construct his Future.

Torkom Saraydarian wrote a large number of books many of which have been published. All of his books will continue to be published and distributed. A few have been translated into Armenian, German, Italian, Spanish, Portuguese, Greek, Dutch, Danish.

He left a rich legacy of writings and musical compositions for all of humanity to enjoy and benefit from for many years to come.

Other Books by Torkom Saraydarian

The Ageless Wisdom
The Bhagavad Gita
Battling Dark Forces
Breakthrough to Higher Psychism
Buddha Sutra — A Dialogue with the Glorious One
Challenge for Discipleship
Christ, The Avatar of Sacrificial Love
A Commentary on Psychic Energy
Cosmic Shocks
Cosmos in Man
The Creative Fire
Dynamics of Success
The Flame of Beauty, Culture, Love, Joy
The Flame of the Heart
From My Heart - Vol. I (Poetry)
Hiawatha and the Great Peace
The Hidden Glory of the Inner Man
I Was
Joy and Healing
Leadership Vol. I
Leadership Vol. II
Leadership Vol. III
Legend of Shamballa
The Mystery of Self-Image
The Mysteries of Willpower
New Dimensions in Healing
Olympus World Report . . . The Year 3000
One Hundred Names of God
Other Worlds
The Psyche and Psychism (Two Volume Set)
The Psychology of Cooperation and Group Consciousness

The Purpose of Life
The Science of Becoming Oneself
The Science of Meditation
The Sense of Responsibility in Society
Sex, Family, and the Woman in Society
The Solar Angel
Spiritual Regeneration
The Subconscious Mind and the Chalice
Symphony of the Zodiac
Talks on Agni
Thought and the Glory of Thinking
Triangles of Fire
Unusual Court
Woman, Torch of the Future
The Year 2000 & After

Booklets
A Daily Discipline of Worship
The Art of Visualization - Simply Presented
Cornerstones of Health
Daily Spiritual Striving
Duties of Grandparents
Earthquakes and Disasters, What the
　Ageless Wisdom Tells Us
Fiery Carriage and Drugs
Five Great Mantrams of the New Age
Hierarchy and the Plan
How to Find Your Level of Meditation
Inner Blooming
Irritation — The Destructive Fire
Mental Exercises
Nachiketas
New Beginnings
Practical Spirituality
Questioning Traveler and Karma
Saint Sergius
Spring of Prosperity
Synthesis

Booklets (Excerpts and Compilations)

- Angels and Devas
- Building Family Unity
- Courage
- First Steps Toward Freedom
- Responsibility
- Responsibility and Business
- Responsibilities of Fathers
- Responsibilities of Mothers
- Prayers, Mantrams & Invocations
- The Psychology of Cooperation
- Success
- The Chalice in Agni Yoga Literature
- Torchbearers
- What to Look for in the Heart of Your Partner

Music (Composed and Performed by Torkom Saraydarian)

- A Touch of Heart (CD) Piano
- Dance of the Zodiac (Cassette) Solo Piano
- Far Horizons (Cassette) Solo Piano
- Fire Blossom (Cassette) Solo Piano
- Infinity (Cassette) Solo Piano
- Lao Tse (Cassette) Solo Piano
- Light Years Ahead (Cassette) Solo Piano
- Lily in Tibet (Cassette) Solo Piano
- Misty Mountains (Cassette) Solo Piano
- Piano Compositions (Cassette)
- Rainbow (Cassette) Solo Piano & Cello
- Spirit of My Heart (Cassette) Voice & Multi-instrument
- Sun Rhythms (Cassette) Oud, Cello, Drum
- Tears of My Joy (Cassette) Solo Piano

• • •

Go In Beauty (Cassette) - 19 Mantrams & Songs Sung by AEG Choir

Videos

The Seven Rays Interpreted
(Video interview with Torkom Saraydarian regarding *The Great Invocation* and the Seven Rays)

Video Lecture Tapes by Torkom Saraydarian
(Audio lecture tapes also available)

Ordering Information

Write to the publisher for additional information regarding:

— Free catalog of author's books and music tapes
— Audio lecture tapes and videos; complete list available
— Placement on mailing list
— New releases and recent information
— A free copy of our newsletter *Outreach*

Additional copies of -

Daily Spiritual Striving
U.S. $6.00
Postage within U.S.A. – $3.00
Plus applicable state sales tax
International postage: contact us for rates
(Specify air or surface mail)

T.S.G. Publishing Foundation, Inc.
P. O. Box 7068
Cave Creek, AZ 85327-7068
United States of America
TEL: (602) 502-1909
FAX: (602) 502-0713

T.S.G. Publishing Foundation, Inc. is a non-profit, tax exempt organization.

Our purpose is to be a pathway for self-transformation. We offer books, audio and video tapes, classes and seminars, and home study courses based on the core values and higher principles of the Ageless Wisdom.

These fine books have been published by the generous donations of the students of the Ageless Wisdom.

Your tax deductible contributions will help us continue publishing and growing.

Our gratitude to all.